40 DAY LIVING

A JOURNEY OF FAITH

40 DAY LIVING

IN THIS ECONOMY

ZENA CONTRERAS

40 Day Living
Published by:
Intermedia Publishing Group, Inc.
P.O. Box 2825
Peoria, Arizona 85380
www.intermediapub.com

Copyright © 2011 by Zena Contreras.

ISBN: 978-1-935906-91-9

Scripture quotations are taken from the Holy Bible, New Living Translation. Copyright

2005 Used by permission of Tyndale.

You can contact the Author on the Internet at www.zenacontreras.com

This book was printed in the United States of America.

Contents

You can contact the author on the Internet at *www.zenacontreras.com*

Introduction

I moved to Arizona from California in search of peace, "seek and you shall find." Less than ten years ago, I was facing a very similar crisis as a result of the dot-com crash. On looking back, I thought I had learned my lesson, but time permits one to forget and move on or maybe just move around.

It's funny how life repeats itself, regardless of the invitation. The core situation is the same: just different players, environment, and circumstances, yet they are all the same.

As a successful recruiter for the last twenty years, I hired and trained thousands, but while I was busy climbing the (invisible) corporate ladder, I lost sight of me and my God. I was routinely attending church, praying when I remembered, speaking a word of truth (occasionally), and here I am lost yet again.

And that's where this book began, in a heart yearning for God and surrendering to His Will, forsaking life as I had known it to be. Sure it is easy to seek God in the midst of a crisis, but my journey began in my early years when life was productive and prosperous.

Always spiritual even while I was a practicing Catholic, I knew of God but also thought that it was my life to control. And that's why history continued to repeat in my life. What I thought was the image of a good God-fearing person was merely my mask with a little routine for good measure.

Faith was not something I thought much about because my feeble mind assumed . . . it was a given. Just like on a Sunday: stand, sit, kneel, sit, stand, and leave. I am not knocking the catholic faith, merely expressing my experience. I was in a rut with my spirituality and my relationship with God.

My move to Arizona left me without a home church and the motivation to find one right away. Nevertheless, there are always my nightly prayers. All the time, I bartered with God, and all the while, He continued to call me closer with new experiences and opportunities to grow yet, I only saw chaos and confusion. Never realizing it was a "calling" for humitlity, change and growth.

So here I am again in the midst of a crisis and a mental meltdown. Yet, this time I did not want to try to figure it out, by myself. To be honest, that wasn't working out all that well! Prayer and conversations with God are more frequent, but it is only when I can become still and listen that I find the peace I had always been in search of, even in this economy or better known as a recession. Yes, it was peace that carried me through another financial setback, spriritual and personal crisis while in the middle of foreclosure.

This economy shook the core of everything I had owned and thought I was. I was unemployed again yet this time with a new home and a mortgage. Eleven months went by and I tried everything, again trying to fix the problem. Sure I prayed, but my prayers were becoming more of a plea than prayers of gratitude and grace. My knees ached for the moments I often dropped in a cry for help.

I am a good person. Why is this happening to me (again)? What have I done wrong? I was pleading like a child after throwing a tantrum. All the while God heard my prayers the first time; what He did not receive was my faith and I was unsure of how to turn things around. Faith was never taught to me but spoken of, as something I could find at any given moment. However, I must have been searching in all the wrong directions because I had very little in my forty plus years of life.

In the throes of turmoil, I started to seek God's wisdom by reading the Bible. Looking for guidance at every turn of the page, I slowly but surely found my mustard seed of faith. Reading God's promises and learning about the sacrifice Jesus made for me gave me hope and courage to endure another day.

As time passed, I found my peace again, but this time, it was like never before. It was something so different, pure, and indescribable in any words. This peace sustained me even as I moved all of my belongings out of the home that I had lost. This peace sustained when I explained to my sons that I had lost my home and was in the middle of another crisis yet this time was very different. This time with conviction, I knew my journey was different and this setback would not repeat in my life again. This time peace sustains me while I seek nothing but God.

It was this peace that prompted me to write and share with others. Surely, many others were in the midst of a meltdown, crisis, foreclosure, and/or a job loss. In moments of nothingness, we can all discover our fullness and purpose. It is in this very moment that we have to make a choice for our own self and others.

This season is an assignment in my life that I had to go through in order to share my experience with the intention and purpose to help and be of service to others!

Instruction

This book is designed like a journal with scriptures, meditation, and a daily call to action. It is designed to help you see God's promise and take action in your life.

Each day, you will be called to act upon an intention. In all such journeys in life there are moments of reflection. This book will allow you to stop along the way and communicate what you are experiencing. Your writings are your communication with God.

The hardest battle to win is the one in the mind of a hopeless person. The rage of war that has left many battle scars is seen in the eyes and the souls of many. It is this hopelessness that many experience when their (perceived) foundation is being shaken with the violent effects of an uncertain economy and future.

Chapters three through ten are filled with selected scriptures to help you with managing your mind. Each day, you will be prompted to a specific call to action that may or may not be related to your current situation. The call to action allows you to expand into a space of giving, receiving, reflecting and knowing. Close each day with the meditative scripture. Or, when the crazy effects of your situation are too much for you, find a place to close your eyes and mediate, even if for a few seconds.

Chapter eleven is filled with God's promises and answers to problems. Some may be the very answer He has for you regarding your situation. And chapter twelve is designed to be used as a tool and expression for your very intimate, direct conversations with God. Chapter twelve can also be used to document your commitment to another 40 days.

While I do not profess to be a theologian or a master teacher of the Bible scripture, the scriptures used in this book resonated with me while I was in the throes of my crisis. However, what was experienced through the repetition of repeated prayers and meditation on specific scriptures was clarity of God's Promises.

This journey of faith is not done as a conclusion to all of one's prayers being answered at the end of the forty days. Yet it is the beginning of a lifetime of commitment to faith. The first forty days will be challenging, and you may or may not complete all the actions, but rest assured you will *receive* as a result of your efforts.

It is encouraged to take the journey again and again. Your life will change when you devote time to worship and communicate with God. Clarity is the first blessing of receivership. This is not a trial membership with a designated destination or prize at the end of the time frame, *it is your life!*

Chapter One

Effects of the Economy

The first decade of the twenty-first century brought about many trials and countless tribulations. Starting with the fear of midnight December 31, 1999, people pulled all their money out of banks and stocked up on supplies, food, and water—preparing for the worst. Then January 1, 2000, rolled around and the sun came up as usual and no major catastrophes occurred.

On September 11, 2001, the world stood still, watching the horrific terrorist attack on the World Trade Center. Shock filled the air and paralyzed the masses, city to city, state to state, nation to nation; we all feared what could happen next. Americans were overwhelmed with emotions. Fear and anger came knocking at the doorsteps of the United States. How could this happen? The reality was it had been happening for many years in other parts of the world.

Arrogance and ignorance had been the veil covering many. People were enraged and emotions were boiling over at any rash comment or indifference. Everyone lived on full alert, and many were singled out for the mere color of their skin. American pride was the badge of honor worn by many giving way to the desire to defend and fight against any perceived threat, regardless of its merit.

Next was the exposure of sheer greed of the many white-collar giants that would topple our financial foundation for many years to come. Billions were made and pocketed by some. Much was stolen, and the population of nations faced a plague knocking at their doors like no other. Financial uncertainty attracted desperation like bees to honey, i.e. killer bees.

Those in positions of power would make decisions that would impact generations to come. The life most knew soon disappeared, never to return. Families had to adjust and getting back to the basics became the norm. Food banks became commonplace as a family's food source. Neighborhoods turned over, and the sounds of kids playing in the streets became silent in some areas. Suicides and family tragedies were on the rise. Rather than seeking God for resolve, some people filled with shame and racked with anxiety, decided to take matters into their own hands. Many lives would never be the same once the feeling of hopelessness settled in and took hold.

This economy, although different than other recessions, had one similarity . . . fear. Fear invaded the souls and crippled the hopes of many. It was on a mission to take a census of each household and capture the most personal details, only to be used against us at just the right moment.

While millions remain unemployed and billions are being spent on unemployment benefits, people are lost, broken with no sight of healing or hope. To you, I say open your eyes, drop to your knees with folded hands, and pray. Prayer will change, praise will ease, but faith will restore beyond belief.

Chapter Two

Why Me? Why Now?

Why me and why now? How could this be happening? There is no magic pill, potion, or person who could answer this question for you. No employer, spouse, friend, or family member could, should, or would truthfully answer this question for you. The only source and answer is the *only source . . . God.* He did not do this to you and is not testing you for a destination or purpose.

However, the truth lies in the question, and the answer is revealed when you stop asking. Nothing that has not happened to someone else is happening to you . . . you are not alone. What is happening is happening through you to give birth to something new within you.

The real reality is that you played a part in this situation. Ok, forgive me for telling the truth, but if you are offended, stop reading right now because you are not ready for your prayers to be answered. If I have offended you, and you are taken aback by the statement and have not acknowledged your part in this crisis, you have the wrong book.

This book is about God's promises and the action needed to propel your faith into the divine receivership and blessings. It is a journey of *your* faith and a testimony that you will share with others. I once heard Juanita Bynum say, "if you don't know my pain you will never understand my praise." We are all here in the flesh as a representation of God and our soul-job is to glorify him in our works, relationships, family but most in our praise.

Why you? Why now? Because God is calling you to a deeper level of understanding and be a witness of what is to be. You are His child, and He has never left or forsaken you. This is temporal and was never in His plan for you. However, somewhere along the way you became sidetracked and lost sight of His will. His plan was always to use you as a testimony for the benefit of others and to bear witness to His ability.

Maybe there is something you imposed upon yourself, took from another, forgot to say, acted out, took a short cut to get, forgot to pay, intended to do, manipulated, cheated, lied, or just did not want to waste your time; and now this has manifested into the personal effects of the economic downturn in your life.

God is not keeping a list of who is bad or good, who should be affected, and who should not be affected. No one is sitting in Heaven saying, "approved, denied or revoked." It has always been your time, the right time; and in this very moment, you can create change.

We are all evolving, and our livelihood is experiencing a shift. The real question is; how do we adapt to what is happening? Can we make it through or will we resist? What is God trying to show you? What lesson do you need to learn?

For me, why me, why now is about my growth and an expansion of my faith in God. About surrendering my old ways of doing and resolving things and allowing His Will to prevail. A release from the distractions of life and a celebration of inner peace. A knowing and believing that all will be well regardless of the appearance.

In my quest for answer to the troubles of this economy, I was drawn to this scripture, which clearly describes a crisis of many sorts:

Why Me, Why Now?

What sorrow for you who buy up house after house and field after field, until everyone is evicted and you live alone in the land? But I have heard the Lord of Heaven's Armies swear a solemn oath: "Many houses will stand deserted; even beautiful mansions will be empty. Ten acres of vineyard will not produce even six gallons of wine. Ten baskets of seed will yield only one basket of grain."

What sorrow for those who get up early in the morning looking for a drink of alcohol and spend long evenings drinking wine to make themselves flaming drunk. They furnish wine and lovely music at their grand parties—lyre and harp, tambourine and flute—but they never think about the Lord or notice what he is doing.

(Isaiah. 5:8-10)

Why you? Why now?

How has this economy affected your life and the life of your family?

_____
_____
_____
_____
_____
_____
_____
_____
_____

How are you living right now?

_____
_____
_____
_____
_____
_____
_____

Why Me, Why Now?

What changes need to occur immediately?

_____

_____

_____

_____

_____

_____

_____

_____

_____

_____

Chapter Three

Do Not Be Afraid

Reading:

He said, "Listen, all you people of Judah and Jerusalem! Listen, King
Jehoshaphat! This is what the Lord says: Do not be afraid! Don't be
discouraged by this mighty army, for the battle is not yours, but God's.

Tomorrow, march out against them. You will find them coming up
through the ascent of Ziz at the end of the valley that opens into the
wilderness of Jeruel.

But you will not even need to fight. Take your positions; then stand
still and watch the Lord's victory. He is with you, O people of Judah
and Jerusalem. Do not be afraid or discouraged. Go out against them
tomorrow, for the Lord is with you!"
(2 Chronicles 20:15-17)

Do Not Be Afraid

Day 1

Call to Action:

Today what are your fears?

What you fear is merely an illusion of what you are seeing as today's reality. God's reality for your life is no illusion but His promise to you. Unlike the false guarantees of the visible world, His invisible Power will provide, protect, and prosper.

Reflection:

_____

_____

_____

_____

_____

_____

_____

_____

_____

_____

Do Not Be Afraid

Prayer:

The Lord is my shepherd; I have all that I need. He lets me rest in green
meadows; he leads me beside peaceful streams. He renews my strength.
He guides me along right paths, bringing honor to his name. Even when
I walk through the darkest valley, I will not be afraid, for you are close
besides me. Your rod and your staff protect and comfort me. You prepare
a feast for me in the presence of my enemies. You honor me by anointing
my head with oil. Surely your goodness and unfailing love will pursue
me all the days of my life, and I will live in the house of the Lord forever.
(Psalm 23:1-6)

Prayer Journal
God is never silent. He is always speaking to you . . . Be still and listen.

Meditation:

God is our refuge and strength, always ready to help in times of trouble.
(Psalm 46:1)

Exceptations

Day 2

Reading:

See how very much our Father loves us, for he calls us his children,
and that is what we are! But the people who belong to this world don't
recognize that we are God's children because they don't know him.

Dear friends, we are already God's children, but he has not yet shown us
what we will be like when Christ appears. But we do know that we will
be like him, for we will see him as he really is.

And all who have this eager expectation will keep themselves pure,
just as he is pure.
(1 John 3:1-3)

Expectations

Day 2

Call to Action:

Today, what expectations do you have for your future in this economy?

How can changing your expectations change your outcome?

In the midst of crisis, we often lower our expectations because of the unanswered prayers. Know that if God heard your prayers, they *will* be answered. Raise your expectations and watch God show up and show out in your life.

Reflection:

_____
_____
_____
_____
_____
_____
_____
_____
_____
_____

Expectations

Day 2

Prayer:

The Lord is my shepherd; I have all that I need. He lets me rest in green
meadows; he leads me beside peaceful streams. He renews my strength.
He guides me along right paths, bringing honor to his name. Even when
I walk through the darkest valley, I will not be afraid, for you are close
besides me. Your rod and your staff protect and comfort me. You prepare
a feast for me in the presence of my enemies. You honor me by anointing
my head with oil. Surely your goodness and unfailing love will pursue
me all the days of my life, and I will live in the house of the Lord forever.
(Psalm 23:1-6)

Prayer Journal
God is never silent. He is always speaking to you . . . Be still and listen.

_____
_____
_____
_____
_____
_____
_____
_____
_____
_____

Meditation:

God is our refuge and strength, always ready to help in times of trouble.
(Psalm 46:1)

Eager to Do Good

Reading:

For the Scriptures say,

If you want to enjoy life and see many happy days, keep your tongue
from speaking evil and your lips from telling lies.

Turn away from evil and do good. Search for peace,
and work to maintain it.

The eyes of the Lord watch over those who do right, and his ears are open
to their prayers. But the Lord turns his face against those who do evil.

Now, who will want to harm you if you are eager to do good?

But even if you suffer for doing what is right, God will reward you for it.
So don't worry or be afraid of their threats.

Instead, you must worship Christ as Lord of your life. And if
someone asks about your Christian hope, always be ready to explain it.
(1 Peter 3:10-15)

Eager to Do Good

Day 3

Call to Action:

Today, what are you suffering from the most in your life?

How are you eager to do good in your life and what changes need to be made?

If we move throughout our day being eager to do good (one simple action at a time), good will be drawn to us like a magnet is drawn to metal.

Reflection:

_____

_____

_____

_____

_____

_____

_____

_____

_____

_____

Eager to Do Good

Day 3

Prayer:

The Lord is my shepherd; I have all that I need. He lets me rest in green meadows; he leads me beside peaceful streams. He renews my strength. He guides me along right paths, bringing honor to his name. Even when I walk through the darkest valley, I will not be afraid, for you are close besides me. Your rod and your staff protect and comfort me. You prepare a feast for me in the presence of my enemies. You honor me by anointing my head with oil. Surely your goodness and unfailing love will pursue me all the days of my life, and I will live in the house of the Lord forever.
(Psalm 23:1-6)

Prayer Journal
God is never silent. He is always speaking to you . . . Be still and listen.

_____
_____
_____
_____
_____
_____
_____
_____
_____
_____

Meditation:

God is our refuge and strength, always ready to help in times of trouble.
(Psalm 46:1)

Knocked Down

Day 4

Reading:

For God, who said, "Let there be light in the darkness," has made this light shine in our hearts so we could know the glory of God that is seen in the face of Jesus Christ.

We now have this light shining in our hearts, but we ourselves are like fragile clay jars containing this great treasure. This makes it clear that our great power is from God, not from ourselves.

We are pressed on every side by troubles, but we are not crushed. We are perplexed, but not driven to despair.

We are hunted down, but never abandoned by God. We get knocked down, but we are not destroyed.

Through suffering, our bodies continue to share in the death of Jesus so that the life of Jesus may also be seen in our bodies.
(2 Corinthians 4:6-10)

Knocked Down

Day 4

Call to Action:

Today, how do you feel knocked down by the current economy? Know that if you can look up, you can get up . . . !

Babies have to fall many times before they can learn to walk. Even when they hold on to an object to stand, they will eventually fall. They are strengthened each time they attempt to get up.

Take time to watch an infant learning to walk and know that when you are knocked down, you too gain strength each time you attempt to get up.

Reflection:

_____
_____
_____
_____
_____
_____
_____
_____
_____
_____

Knocked Down

Prayer:

The Lord is my shepherd; I have all that I need. He lets me rest in green
meadows; he leads me beside peaceful streams. He renews my strength.
He guides me along right paths, bringing honor to his name. Even when
I walk through the darkest valley, I will not be afraid, for you are close
besides me. Your rod and your staff protect and comfort me. You prepare
a feast for me in the presence of my enemies. You honor me by anointing
my head with oil. Surely your goodness and unfailing love will pursue
me all the days of my life, and I will live in the house of the Lord forever.
(Psalm 23:1-6)

Prayer Journal
God is never silent. He is always speaking to you . . . Be still and listen.

Meditation:

God is our refuge and strength, always ready to help in times of trouble.
(Psalm 46:1)

Renewed Spirit

Day 5

Reading:

That is why we never give up. Though our bodies are dying, our spirits are being renewed every day.

For our present troubles are small and won't last very long. Yet they produce for us a glory that vastly outweighs them and will last forever!

So we don't look at the troubles we can see now; rather, we fix our gaze on things that cannot be seen. For the things we see now will soon be gone, but the things we cannot see will last forever.
(2 Corinthians 4:16-18)

Renewed Spirit

Day 5

Call to Action:

Today, how can you renew your spirit?

What are you willing to change to have a renewed spiritual experience?

Renewing is a part of change, and change is needed to grow spiritually.

Reflection:

_____

_____

_____

_____

_____

_____

_____

_____

_____

_____

Renewed Spirit

Day 5

Prayer:

The Lord is my shepherd; I have all that I need. He lets me rest in green
meadows; he leads me beside peaceful streams. He renews my strength.
He guides me along right paths, bringing honor to his name. Even when
I walk through the darkest valley, I will not be afraid, for you are close
besides me. Your rod and your staff protect and comfort me. You prepare
a feast for me in the presence of my enemies. You honor me by anointing
my head with oil. Surely your goodness and unfailing love will pursue
me all the days of my life, and I will live in the house of the Lord forever.
(Psalm 23:1-6)

Prayer Journal
God is never silent. He is always speaking to you . . . Be still and listen.

Meditation:

God is our refuge and strength, always ready to help in times of trouble.
(Psalm 46:1)

Revelations

What is being revealed to you? How has God shown up in your life?

_____

_____

_____

_____

_____

_____

_____

_____

_____

_____

_____

_____

_____

_____

_____

_____

_____

_____

_____

_____

_____

_____

_____

_____

_____

_____

_____

_____

He was the one who prayed to the God of Israel, "Oh, that you would
bless me and expand my territory! Please be with me in all that I do, and
keep me from all trouble and pain!" And God granted him his request.
(1 Chronicles 4:10)

Chapter Four

Clear Mind

Day 6

Reading:

But you should keep a clear mind in every situation. Don't be afraid of suffering for the Lord. Work at telling others the Good News, and fully carry out the ministry God has given you.
(2 Timothy 4:5)

Clear Mind

Day 6

Call to Action:

Today, stop the crazy "monkey chatter" in your mind by releasing those negative thoughts as quickly as they enter. One way to do this is to give praise for what you have in your life.

What thoughts continue to plague your mind? Write them down, then release them in a praise statement, such as; if you are losing your home the perfect praise-statement would be; I am grateful for God's never-ending shelter. Praise statements or affirmations are a great way to shut down the "monkey chatter" in our minds and can be used as a useful weapon against any negativity.

Reflection:

_____

_____

_____

_____

_____

_____

_____

_____

_____

_____

Clear Mind

Day 6

Prayer:

The Lord is my shepherd; I have all that I need. He lets me rest in green meadows; he leads me beside peaceful streams. He renews my strength. He guides me along right paths, bringing honor to his name. Even when I walk through the darkest valley, I will not be afraid, for you are close besides me. Your rod and your staff protect and comfort me. You prepare a feast for me in the presence of my enemies. You honor me by anointing my head with oil. Surely your goodness and unfailing love will pursue me all the days of my life, and I will live in the house of the Lord forever.
(Psalm 23:1-6)

Prayer Journal
God is never silent. He is always speaking to you . . . Be still and listen.

_____
_____
_____
_____
_____
_____
_____
_____
_____
_____

Meditation:

God is our refuge and strength, always ready to help in times of trouble.
(Psalm 46:1)

Self-Discipline

Day 7

Reading:

For God has not given us a spirit of fear and timidity, but of power, love, and self-discipline.
(2 Timothy 1:7)

Self-Discipline

Day 7

Call to Action:

Today, turn off the TV and practice a little self-discipline from technology. Spend time listening to the wonders of the world around you and take heed of all God's wonderous creations. God's amazing power to create continues to change life as we know it daily.

TV and modern technology have benefited us all, but we need to be disciplined enough to know they have become a distraction and an obsession. People endured many years without cell phone, iPods and computers. God asks for so little yet continues to give so much.

Reflection:

_____

_____

_____

_____

_____

_____

_____

_____

_____

_____

Self-Discipline

Day 7

Prayer:

The Lord is my shepherd; I have all that I need. He lets me rest in green
meadows; he leads me beside peaceful streams. He renews my strength.
He guides me along right paths, bringing honor to his name. Even when
I walk through the darkest valley, I will not be afraid, for you are close
besides me. Your rod and your staff protect and comfort me. You prepare
a feast for me in the presence of my enemies. You honor me by anointing
my head with oil. Surely your goodness and unfailing love will pursue
me all the days of my life, and I will live in the house of the Lord forever.
(Psalm 23:1-6)

Prayer Journal
God is never silent. He is always speaking to you . . . Be still and listen.

_____
_____
_____
_____
_____
_____
_____
_____
_____
_____

Meditation:

God is our refuge and strength, always ready to help in times of trouble.
(Psalm 46:1)

Light in the Darkness

Reading:

Satan, who is the god of this world, has blinded the minds of those who don't believe. They are unable to see the glorious light of the Good News. They don't understand this message about the glory of Christ, who is the exact likeness of God.

You see, we don't go around preaching about ourselves. We preach that Jesus Christ is Lord, and we ourselves are your servants for Jesus' sake.

For God, who said, "Let there be light in the darkness," has made this light shine in our hearts so we could know the glory of God that is seen in the face of Jesus Christ.

We now have this light shining in our hearts, but we ourselves are like fragile clay jars containing this great treasure. This makes it clear that our great power is from God, not from ourselves.
(2 Corinthians 4:4-7)

Light in the Darkness

Day 8

Call to Action:

Today, be the light in the darkness for someone by practicing random acts of kindness. What are you willing to do for someone else today? Then, just do it . . . !

Someone is in need of some kindness today and you can be the blessing they have been in search of. No matter big or small, a single random act of kindness benefits us all!

Reflection:

_____

_____

_____

_____

_____

_____

_____

_____

_____

_____

Light in the Darkness

Prayer:

The Lord is my shepherd; I have all that I need. He lets me rest in green
meadows; he leads me beside peaceful streams. He renews my strength.
He guides me along right paths, bringing honor to his name. Even when
I walk through the darkest valley, I will not be afraid, for you are close
besides me. Your rod and your staff protect and comfort me. You prepare
a feast for me in the presence of my enemies. You honor me by anointing
my head with oil. Surely your goodness and unfailing love will pursue
me all the days of my life, and I will live in the house of the Lord forever.
(Psalm 23:1-6)

Prayer Journal
God is never silent. He is always speaking to you . . . Be still and listen.

_____
_____
_____
_____
_____
_____
_____
_____
_____
_____
_____

Meditation:

God is our refuge and strength, always ready to help in times of trouble.
(Psalm 46:1)

Deliver Me

Day 9

Reading:

The first time I was brought before the judge, no one came with me. Everyone abandoned me. May it not be counted against them.

But the Lord stood with me and gave me strength so that I might preach the Good News in its entirety for all the Gentiles to hear. And he rescued me from certain death.

Yes, and the Lord will deliver me from every evil attack and will bring me safely into his heavenly Kingdom. All glory to God forever and ever! Amen.
(2 Timothy 4:16-18)

Deliver Me

Day 9

Call to Action:

Today, write down how God has *delivered* you through various situations and how you want Him to deliver you through this economical downturn.

Know that God's promises are real and shall never be broken.

Reflection:

_____
_____
_____
_____
_____
_____
_____
_____
_____
_____

Deliver Me

Day 9

Prayer:

The Lord is my shepherd; I have all that I need. He lets me rest in green
meadows; he leads me beside peaceful streams. He renews my strength.
He guides me along right paths, bringing honor to his name. Even when
I walk through the darkest valley, I will not be afraid, for you are close
besides me. Your rod and your staff protect and comfort me. You prepare
a feast for me in the presence of my enemies. You honor me by anointing
my head with oil. Surely your goodness and unfailing love will pursue
me all the days of my life, and I will live in the house of the Lord forever.
(Psalm 23:1-6)

Prayer Journal
God is never silent. He is always speaking to you . . . Be still and listen.

_____

_____

_____

_____

_____

_____

_____

_____

_____

_____

Meditation:

God is our refuge and strength, always ready to help in times of trouble.
(Psalm 46:1)

Give You Rest

Day 10

Reading:

Then Jesus said, "Come to me, all of you who are weary and carry heavy burdens, and I will give you rest.

Take my yoke upon you. Let me teach you, because I am humble and gentle at heart, and you will find rest for your souls.

For my yoke is easy to bear, and the burden I give you is light." (Matthew 11:28-30)

Give You Rest

Day 10

Call to Action:

Today, take time to rest from the cares of the world. No matter what is going on, practice; *seed, time harvest* and do not react or give any attention to the elements burdening you in this economy. You are diligent and have laid seed, now you are in the season of time, patiently waiting for the future harvest.

Something may be trying to reveal itself to you, and you are too busy to see or hear. When you rest, you reenergize and are better prepared for the harvest to come.

How has God given you rest from your burdens?

Reflection:

_____

_____

_____

_____

_____

_____

_____

_____

_____

Give You Rest

Prayer:

The Lord is my shepherd; I have all that I need. He lets me rest in green
meadows; he leads me beside peaceful streams. He renews my strength.
He guides me along right paths, bringing honor to his name. Even when
I walk through the darkest valley, I will not be afraid, for you are close
besides me. Your rod and your staff protect and comfort me. You prepare
a feast for me in the presence of my enemies. You honor me by anointing
my head with oil. Surely your goodness and unfailing love will pursue
me all the days of my life, and I will live in the house of the Lord forever.
(Psalm 23:1-6)

Prayer Journal
God is never silent. He is always speaking to you . . . Be still and listen.

_____

_____

_____

_____

_____

_____

_____

_____

_____

_____

Meditation:

God is our refuge and strength, always ready to help in times of trouble.
(Psalm 46:1)

Revelations

What is being revealed to you? How has God shown up in your life?

_____
_____
_____
_____
_____
_____
_____
_____
_____
_____
_____
_____
_____
_____
_____
_____
_____
_____
_____
_____
_____
_____
_____
_____
_____
_____
_____
_____
_____
_____
_____
_____

He was the one who prayed to the God of Israel, "Oh, that you would
bless me and expand my territory! Please be with me in all that I do, and
keep me from all trouble and pain!" And God granted him his request.
(1 Chronicles 4:10)

Chapter Five

Blessings

Reading:

"If you fully obey the LORD your God and carefully keep all his
commands that I am giving you today, the LORD your God will set you
high above all the nations of the world.

You will experience all these blessings if you obey the LORD your God:

Your towns and your fields will be blessed.

Your children and your crops will be blessed. The offspring of your herds
and flocks will be blessed.

Your fruit baskets and breadboards will be blessed.

Wherever you go and whatever you do, you will be blessed.
(Deuteronomy 28:1-6)

Blessings

Day 11

Call to Action:

Today, recognize the blessings in your life and give thanks for all that you have and are.

How many blessings do you have in your life . . . right now?

We often focus on our problems and trying to find a solution rather than seeing the many blessings that exist in our lives. The art of saying "thank you" is vanishing. Blessings are all around you and be thankful for them all!

Reflection:

_____

_____

_____

_____

_____

_____

_____

_____

_____

Blessings

Day 11

Prayer:

The Lord is my shepherd; I have all that I need. He lets me rest in green
meadows; he leads me beside peaceful streams. He renews my strength.
He guides me along right paths, bringing honor to his name. Even when
I walk through the darkest valley, I will not be afraid, for you are close
besides me. Your rod and your staff protect and comfort me. You prepare
a feast for me in the presence of my enemies. You honor me by anointing
my head with oil. Surely your goodness and unfailing love will pursue
me all the days of my life, and I will live in the house of the Lord forever.
(Psalm 23:1-6)

Prayer Journal
God is never silent. He is always speaking to you . . . Be still and listen.

_____

_____

_____

_____

_____

_____

_____

_____

_____

_____

_____

Meditation:

Wait patiently for the Lord. Be brave and courageous. Yes, wait patiently
for the Lord.
(Psalm 27:14)

Human Body

Day 12

Reading:

Don't let anyone capture you with empty philosophies and high-sounding nonsense that come from human thinking and from the spiritual powers of this world, rather than from Christ.

For in Christ lives all the fullness of God in a human body.

So you also are complete through your union with Christ, who is the head over every ruler and authority.
(Colossians 2:8-10)

Human Body

Day 12

Call to Action:

Today, take special care of your body. Treat yourself to something really special. Take extra pride in your appearance today.

Our bodies are God's temple and we are made in His image and likeness. When we treasure our bodies, we delight God.

Reflection:

_____

_____

_____

_____

_____

_____

_____

_____

_____

_____

Human Body

Day 12

Prayer:

The Lord is my shepherd; I have all that I need. He lets me rest in green
meadows; he leads me beside peaceful streams. He renews my strength.
He guides me along right paths, bringing honor to his name. Even when
I walk through the darkest valley, I will not be afraid, for you are close
besides me. Your rod and your staff protect and comfort me. You prepare
a feast for me in the presence of my enemies. You honor me by anointing
my head with oil. Surely your goodness and unfailing love will pursue
me all the days of my life, and I will live in the house of the Lord forever.
(Psalm 23:1-6)

Prayer Journal
God is never silent. He is always speaking to you . . . Be still and listen.

_____
_____
_____
_____
_____
_____
_____
_____
_____
_____

Meditation:

Wait patiently for the Lord. Be brave and courageous. Yes, wait patiently
for the Lord.
(Psalm 27:14)

Be Bold and Confident

Day 13

Reading:

Because of Christ and our faith in him,

we can now come boldly and

confidently into God's presence.

So please don't lose heart because of my trials here.

I am suffering for you, so you should feel honored.
(Ephesians 3:12-13)

Be Bold and Confident

Day 13

Call to Action:

Today, take a bold action with confidence. Do something that you would never think of doing. Challenge yourself to act in a bold manner regardless of your fears or the desired outcome.

Sometimes parents have to take bold actions in this economy for the sake of their family, regardless of the fears they may have. Parents must appear confident in their decisions. Children may not be aware of the fears some parents have regarding the livelihood and protection their family.

Wimpy actions produce wimpy, measly result. Bold actions taken in confidence produce bold results.

Reflection:

_____

_____

_____

_____

_____

_____

_____

_____

_____

_____

Be Bold and Confident

Day 13

Prayer:

The Lord is my shepherd; I have all that I need. He lets me rest in green
meadows; he leads me beside peaceful streams. He renews my strength.
He guides me along right paths, bringing honor to his name. Even when
I walk through the darkest valley, I will not be afraid, for you are close
besides me. Your rod and your staff protect and comfort me. You prepare
a feast for me in the presence of my enemies. You honor me by anointing
my head with oil. Surely your goodness and unfailing love will pursue
me all the days of my life, and I will live in the house of the Lord forever.
(Psalm 23:1-6)

Prayer Journal
God is never silent. He is always speaking to you . . . Be still and listen.

_____
_____
_____
_____
_____
_____
_____
_____
_____
_____

Meditation:

Wait patiently for the Lord. Be brave and courageous. Yes, wait patiently
for the Lord.
(Psalm 27:14)

Rewards

Day 14

Reading:

It was by faith that Enoch was taken up to heaven without dying—
"he disappeared, because God took him."

For before he was taken up, he was known as a person who pleased God.

And it is impossible to please God without faith. Anyone who wants to
come to him must believe that God exists and that he rewards those who
sincerely seek him.

It was by faith that Noah built a large boat to save his family from the
flood. He obeyed God, who warned him about things that had never
happened before. By his faith Noah condemned the rest of the world, and
he received the righteousness that comes by faith.
(Hebrew 11:5-7)

Rewards

Day 14

Call to Action:

Today, reward someone anonymously, and you will be rewarded for your kind deeds. Take out a neighbor's trash, give someone a treat or a gift . . . just because!

It is the good within you that will be rewarded and used as a testimony of the glory of God.

Reflection:

_____
_____
_____
_____
_____
_____
_____
_____
_____
_____

Rewards

Day 14

Prayer:

The Lord is my shepherd; I have all that I need. He lets me rest in green meadows; he leads me beside peaceful streams. He renews my strength. He guides me along right paths, bringing honor to his name. Even when I walk through the darkest valley, I will not be afraid, for you are close besides me. Your rod and your staff protect and comfort me. You prepare a feast for me in the presence of my enemies. You honor me by anointing my head with oil. Surely your goodness and unfailing love will pursue me all the days of my life, and I will live in the house of the Lord forever.
(Psalm 23:1-6)

Prayer Journal
God is never silent. He is always speaking to you . . . Be still and listen.

_____

_____

_____

_____

_____

_____

_____

_____

_____

Meditation:

Wait patiently for the Lord. Be brave and courageous. Yes, wait patiently for the Lord.
(Psalm 27:14)

Be Strong

Reading:

Even the wilderness and desert will be glad in those days. The wasteland will rejoice and blossom with spring crocuses.

Yes, there will be an abundance of flowers and singing and joy! The deserts will become as green as the mountains of Lebanon, as lovely as Mount Carmel or the plain of Sharon. There the LORD will display his glory, the splendor of our God.

With this news, strengthen those who have tired hands, and encourage those who have weak knees.

Say to those with fearful hearts, "Be strong, and do not fear, for your God is coming to destroy your enemies. He is coming to save you."
(Isaiah 35:1-4)

Be Strong

Day 15

Call to Action:

Today, be strong in your faith, words, and actions. Envision yourself as a real-life hero and imagine that if you were placed in this time and space for *one* purpose, what would it be? How would you feel as a real-life hero?

Each of us are real-life heros, and we are called upon to be strong not just for ourselves but also for others, wherein lies real strength and courage.

Reflection:

_____

_____

_____

_____

_____

_____

_____

_____

_____

_____

Be Strong

Day 15

Prayer:

The Lord is my shepherd; I have all that I need. He lets me rest in green meadows; he leads me beside peaceful streams. He renews my strength. He guides me along right paths, bringing honor to his name. Even when I walk through the darkest valley, I will not be afraid, for you are close besides me. Your rod and your staff protect and comfort me. You prepare a feast for me in the presence of my enemies. You honor me by anointing my head with oil. Surely your goodness and unfailing love will pursue me all the days of my life, and I will live in the house of the Lord forever. (Psalm 23:1-6)

Prayer Journal
God is never silent. He is always speaking to you . . . Be still and listen.

_____

_____

_____

_____

_____

_____

_____

_____

_____

_____

Meditation:

Wait patiently for the Lord. Be brave and courageous. Yes, wait patiently for the Lord. (Psalm 27:14)

Revelations

What is being revealed to you? How has God shown up in your life?

_____

_____

_____

_____

_____

_____

_____

_____

_____

_____

_____

_____

_____

_____

_____

_____

_____

_____

_____

_____

_____

_____

_____

_____

_____

_____

_____

_____

_____

_____

He was the one who prayed to the God of Israel, "Oh, that you would bless me and expand my territory! Please be with me in all that I do, and keep me from all trouble and pain!" And God granted him his request.
(1 Chronicles 4:10)

Chapter Six

New Strength

Reading:

Look up into the heavens. Who created all the stars? He brings them out like an army, one after another, calling each by its name. Because of his great power and incomparable strength, not a single one is missing.

O Jacob, how can you say the LORD does not see your troubles?

O Israel, how can you say God ignores your rights?

Have you never heard? Have you never understood? The LORD is the everlasting God, the Creator of all the earth. He never grows weak or weary. No one can measure the depths of his understanding.

He gives power to the weak and strength to the powerless.

Even youths will become weak and tired, and young men will fall in exhaustion.

But those who trust in the LORD will find new strength. They will soar high on wings like eagles. They will run and not grow weary. They will walk and not faint.
(Isaiah 40:26-31)

New Strength

Day 16

Call to Action:

Today, you will find new strength in yourself by finding and complimenting the strength you see in others. Write a note or a letter to someone and acknowledge their strength.

Acknowledgment is a form of praise and praise will always bring new strength to the discouraged. Lift your hands in praise today and capture the new strength waiting in the midst of this economy.

Reflection:

_____

_____

_____

_____

_____

_____

_____

_____

_____

_____

New Strength

Prayer:

The Lord is my shepherd; I have all that I need. He lets me rest in green
meadows; he leads me beside peaceful streams. He renews my strength.
He guides me along right paths, bringing honor to his name. Even when
I walk through the darkest valley, I will not be afraid, for you are close
besides me. Your rod and your staff protect and comfort me. You prepare
a feast for me in the presence of my enemies. You honor me by anointing
my head with oil. Surely your goodness and unfailing love will pursue
me all the days of my life, and I will live in the house of the Lord forever.
(Psalm 23:1-6)

Prayer Journal
God is never silent. He is always speaking to you . . . Be still and listen.

_____
_____
_____
_____
_____
_____
_____
_____
_____
_____

Meditation:

Wait patiently for the Lord. Be brave and courageous. Yes, wait patiently
for the Lord.
(Psalm 27:14)

Discouraged

Day 17

Reading:

Then Moses called for Joshua, and as all Israel watched, he said to him, "Be strong and courageous! For you will lead these people into the land that the LORD swore to their ancestors he would give them. You are the one who will divide it among them as their grants of land.

Do not be afraid or discouraged, for the LORD will personally go ahead of you. He will be with you; he will neither fail you nor abandon you."
(Deuteronomy 31:7-8)

Discouraged

Day 17

Call to Action:

Today, acknowledge how you have discouraged yourself and others and then do the opposite. Rewrite those moments and see what you could have done or said differently.

We often discourage ourselves from doing something or speaking to someone because of self-doubt. Self-doubt is the villain in every missed opportunity.

Reflection:

_____
_____
_____
_____
_____
_____
_____
_____
_____
_____

Discouraged

Day 17

Prayer:

The Lord is my shepherd; I have all that I need. He lets me rest in green meadows; he leads me beside peaceful streams. He renews my strength. He guides me along right paths, bringing honor to his name. Even when I walk through the darkest valley, I will not be afraid, for you are close besides me. Your rod and your staff protect and comfort me. You prepare a feast for me in the presence of my enemies. You honor me by anointing my head with oil. Surely your goodness and unfailing love will pursue me all the days of my life, and I will live in the house of the Lord forever.
(Psalm 23:1-6)

Prayer Journal
God is never silent. He is always speaking to you . . . Be still and listen.

_____

_____

_____

_____

_____

_____

_____

_____

_____

_____

Meditation:

Wait patiently for the Lord. Be brave and courageous. Yes, wait patiently for the Lord.
(Psalm 27:14)

Credit

Day 18

Reading:

> God saved you by his grace when you believed. And you can't take credit for this; it is a gift from God.
>
> Salvation is not a reward for the good things we have done, so none of us can boast about it.
>
> For we are God's masterpiece. He has created us anew in Christ Jesus, so we can do the good things he planned for us long ago.
> (Ephesians 2:8-10)

Credit

Day 18

Call to Action:

Today, look at your credit score (for a brief moment) and know that it does not define you as a person! Although credit is important, the pursuit of increased credit through the purchase of material possessions (needed or not) is partially to blame for this crisis.

Write a list of all your blessings for each point of your credit score. Give credit to God for all the things that you have and watch your *God*-score increase.

Reflection:

_____

_____

_____

_____

_____

_____

_____

_____

_____

_____

Credit

Prayer:

The Lord is my shepherd; I have all that I need. He lets me rest in green
meadows; he leads me beside peaceful streams. He renews my strength.
He guides me along right paths, bringing honor to his name. Even when
I walk through the darkest valley, I will not be afraid, for you are close
besides me. Your rod and your staff protect and comfort me. You prepare
a feast for me in the presence of my enemies. You honor me by anointing
my head with oil. Surely your goodness and unfailing love will pursue
me all the days of my life, and I will live in the house of the Lord forever.
(Psalm 23:1-6)

Prayer Journal
God is never silent. He is always speaking to you . . . Be still and listen.

_____

_____

_____

_____

_____

_____

_____

_____

_____

_____

Meditation:

Wait patiently for the Lord. Be brave and courageous. Yes, wait patiently
for the Lord.
(Psalm 27:14)

Do Not Panic

Day 19

Reading:

So be strong and courageous!
Do not be afraid and do not panic before them.
For the LORD your God will personally go ahead of you.
He will neither fail you nor abandon you."
(Deuteronomy 31:6)

Do Not Panic

Day 19

Call to Action:

Today, do not panic when you see the appearance of your situation (i.e., bills, finances, family, health, relationships, employment, or unemployment). Be encouraged that God responds to your faith and not to your needs. Your needs may change and be limited, but your faith can always be increased.

Answer this question: If all my needs were met, how would my faith be different?

Reflection:

_____

_____

_____

_____

_____

_____

_____

_____

_____

_____

Do Not Panic

Day 19

Prayer:

The Lord is my shepherd; I have all that I need. He lets me rest in green
meadows; he leads me beside peaceful streams. He renews my strength.
He guides me along right paths, bringing honor to his name. Even when
I walk through the darkest valley, I will not be afraid, for you are close
besides me. Your rod and your staff protect and comfort me. You prepare
a feast for me in the presence of my enemies. You honor me by anointing
my head with oil. Surely your goodness and unfailing love will pursue
me all the days of my life, and I will live in the house of the Lord forever.
(Psalm 23:1-6)

Prayer Journal
God is never silent. He is always speaking to you . . . Be still and listen.

_____
_____
_____
_____
_____
_____
_____
_____
_____
_____

Meditation:

Wait patiently for the Lord. Be brave and courageous. Yes, wait patiently
for the Lord.
(Psalm 27:14)

Prune the Branches

Reading:

"I am the true grapevine, and my Father is the gardener.

He cuts off every branch of mine that doesn't produce fruit, and he prunes the branches that do bear fruit so they will produce even more.

You have already been pruned and purified by the message
I have given you.

Remain in me, and I will remain in you. For a branch cannot produce fruit if it is severed from the vine, and you cannot be fruitful unless you remain in me.
(John 15:1-4)

Prune the Branches

Call to Action:

Today, clean out your closet. Get rid of all the items you have not used or cannot wear and donate them to charity. Do not sell them on eBay or in a yard sale, for it is in giving that one receives. Releasing the old will free up space for all the newness that is to come into your life.

No matter the climate, region, or type of tree, they all need to be pruned in order to continue to grow. Some trees are "self-pruning" or "natural pruning" as known in the scientific world. Be like a tree and self-prune your environment today.

Reflection:

_____

_____

_____

_____

_____

_____

_____

_____

_____

_____

Prune the Branches

Day 20

Prayer:

The Lord is my shepherd; I have all that I need. He lets me rest in green
meadows; he leads me beside peaceful streams. He renews my strength.
He guides me along right paths, bringing honor to his name. Even when
I walk through the darkest valley, I will not be afraid, for you are close
besides me. Your rod and your staff protect and comfort me. You prepare
a feast for me in the presence of my enemies. You honor me by anointing
my head with oil. Surely your goodness and unfailing love will pursue
me all the days of my life, and I will live in the house of the Lord forever.
(Psalm 23:1-6)

Prayer Journal
God is never silent. He is always speaking to you . . . Be still and listen.

_____

_____

_____

_____

_____

_____

_____

_____

_____

_____

Meditation:

Wait patiently for the Lord. Be brave and courageous. Yes, wait patiently
for the Lord.
(Psalm 27:14)

Revelations

What is being revealed to you? How has God shown up in your life?

_____

_____

_____

_____

_____

_____

_____

_____

_____

_____

_____

_____

_____

_____

_____

_____

_____

_____

_____

_____

_____

_____

_____

_____

_____

_____

_____

_____

He was the one who prayed to the God of Israel, "Oh, that you would
bless me and expand my territory! Please be with me in all that I do, and
keep me from all trouble and pain!" And God granted him his request.
(1 Chronicles 4:10)

Chapter Seven

Created

Reading:

This is the written account of Adam's line.

When God created man, he made him in the likeness of God.

He created them male and female and blessed them.

And when they were created, he called them "man.
(Genesis 5:1-2)

Created

Call to Action:

Today, start to build your ideal life by creating a vision of your desires. Collect several pictures and images of what you want in your life and create a vision board. We can only receive what the mind perceives.

Home Builders need a multitude of staff to build new homes. They have to hire engineers, designers, suppliers, builders, and a host of people in operations. Isn't it wonderful to know that you only have to rely on *one* Source and Supplier for all your needs.

What do you need to create the life you desire? Take a moment to craft your ideal life.

Reflection:

_____

_____

_____

_____

_____

_____

_____

_____

_____

_____

Created

Prayer:

The Lord is my shepherd; I have all that I need. He lets me rest in green
meadows; he leads me beside peaceful streams. He renews my strength.
He guides me along right paths, bringing honor to his name. Even when
I walk through the darkest valley, I will not be afraid, for you are close
besides me. Your rod and your staff protect and comfort me. You prepare
a feast for me in the presence of my enemies. You honor me by anointing
my head with oil. Surely your goodness and unfailing love will pursue
me all the days of my life, and I will live in the house of the Lord forever.
(Psalm 23:1-6)

Prayer Journal
God is never silent. He is always speaking to you . . . Be still and listen.

_____

_____

_____

_____

_____

_____

_____

_____

_____

_____

Meditation:

In my desperation I prayed, and the Lord listened; he saved me from all
my troubles.
(Psalm 34:6)

Intentions

Day 22

Reading:

> But Joseph replied, "Don't be afraid of me. Am I God,
> that I can punish you?
>
> You intended to harm me, but God intended it all for good. He brought
> me to this position so I could save the lives of many people.
>
> No, don't be afraid. I will continue to take care of you and your children."
> So he reassured them by speaking kindly to them.
> (Genesis. 50:19-21)

Intentions

Day 22

Call to Action:

Today, take inventory of your intentions. Are your motives selfish, self-defeating, envious, or misleading? Write down a list of your intentions.

Some people make promises to God, such as, God if you bless me; I will do this . . . or that . . .

Conditional intentions are a form of manipulation and are sinful in God's eyes.

Reflection:

_____

_____

_____

_____

_____

_____

_____

_____

_____

_____

_____

Intentions

Day 22

Prayer:

The Lord is my shepherd; I have all that I need. He lets me rest in green
meadows; he leads me beside peaceful streams. He renews my strength.
He guides me along right paths, bringing honor to his name. Even when
I walk through the darkest valley, I will not be afraid, for you are close
besides me. Your rod and your staff protect and comfort me. You prepare
a feast for me in the presence of my enemies. You honor me by anointing
my head with oil. Surely your goodness and unfailing love will pursue
me all the days of my life, and I will live in the house of the Lord forever.
(Psalm 23:1-6)

Prayer Journal
God is never silent. He is always speaking to you . . . Be still and listen.

_____
_____
_____
_____
_____
_____
_____
_____
_____
_____

Meditation:

In my desperation I prayed, and the Lord listened; he saved me from all
my troubles.
(Psalm 34:6)

Enemies

Reading:

"Don't ever be afraid or discouraged," Joshua told his men.

"Be strong and courageous,

for the LORD is going to do this to all of your enemies."
(Joshua 10:25)

Enemies

Day 23

Call to Action:

Today, write list of people who you view are your enemies or have wronged you and *forgive them*! Even if you forgive them in silence, you are releasing the negativity of the past and opening yourself to future blessings. Maybe someone is forgiving you right now!

Reflection:

_____

_____

_____

_____

_____

_____

_____

_____

_____

_____

Enemies

Day 23

Prayer:

The Lord is my shepherd; I have all that I need. He lets me rest in green
meadows; he leads me beside peaceful streams. He renews my strength.
He guides me along right paths, bringing honor to his name. Even when
I walk through the darkest valley, I will not be afraid, for you are close
besides me. Your rod and your staff protect and comfort me. You prepare
a feast for me in the presence of my enemies. You honor me by anointing
my head with oil. Surely your goodness and unfailing love will pursue
me all the days of my life, and I will live in the house of the Lord forever.
(Psalm 23:1-6)

Prayer Journal
God is never silent. He is always speaking to you . . . Be still and listen.

_____
_____
_____
_____
_____
_____
_____
_____
_____
_____

Meditation:

In my desperation I prayed, and the Lord listened; he saved me from all
my troubles.
(Psalm 34:6)

His Plan

Day 24

Reading:

This is what the Lord says: "You will be in Babylon for seventy years. But then I will come and do for you all the good things I have promised, and I will bring you home again.

For I know the plans I have for you," says the Lord. "They are plans for good and not for disaster, to give you a future and a hope.

In those days when you pray, I will listen.
(Jeremiah 29:10-12)

His Plan

Day 24

Call to Action:

Today, recognize your planning or lack there of; is in direct correlation to your current situation. When we focus on our plan and not on God's plan for our life, we very well may be contributing to the crisis and our economical downturn.

It is when we try to control everything that we are least in control. Write down all the things you are willing to surrender to God. "Thy will be done."

Reflection:

_____

_____

_____

_____

_____

_____

_____

_____

_____

_____

His Plan

Day 24

Prayer:

The Lord is my shepherd; I have all that I need. He lets me rest in green
meadows; he leads me beside peaceful streams. He renews my strength.
He guides me along right paths, bringing honor to his name. Even when
I walk through the darkest valley, I will not be afraid, for you are close
besides me. Your rod and your staff protect and comfort me. You prepare
a feast for me in the presence of my enemies. You honor me by anointing
my head with oil. Surely your goodness and unfailing love will pursue
me all the days of my life, and I will live in the house of the Lord forever.
(Psalm 23:1-6)

Prayer Journal
God is never silent. He is always speaking to you . . . Be still and listen.

_____

_____

_____

_____

_____

_____

_____

_____

_____

_____

Meditation:

In my desperation I prayed, and the Lord listened; he saved me from all
my troubles.
(Psalm 34:6)

Listening

Day 25

Reading:

"Anyone who listens to my teaching and follows it is wise, like a person
who builds a house on solid rock.

Though the rain comes in torrents and the floodwaters rise and the winds
beat against that house, it won't collapse because it is built on bedrock.

But anyone who hears my teaching and doesn't obey it is foolish, like a
person who builds a house on sand.

When the rains and floods come and the winds beat against that house,
it will collapse with a mighty crash."
(Matthew 7:24-27)

Listening

Call to Action:

Today, take a moment to listen to what God is trying to say to you.

Listen intently; oftentimes when God speaks to us and we misinterpret it to be our imagination. We need to learn how to listen and discern when God is speaking or blessing us with a spiritual-seed.

What messages or spiritual-seeds have you missed because you are too focused on your situation?

Reflection:

_____
_____
_____
_____
_____
_____
_____
_____
_____
_____

Listening

Prayer:

The Lord is my shepherd; I have all that I need. He lets me rest in green
meadows; he leads me beside peaceful streams. He renews my strength.
He guides me along right paths, bringing honor to his name. Even when
I walk through the darkest valley, I will not be afraid, for you are close
besides me. Your rod and your staff protect and comfort me. You prepare
a feast for me in the presence of my enemies. You honor me by anointing
my head with oil. Surely your goodness and unfailing love will pursue
me all the days of my life, and I will live in the house of the Lord forever.
(Psalm 23:1-6)

Prayer Journal
God is never silent. He is always speaking to you . . . Be still and listen.

_____
_____
_____
_____
_____
_____
_____
_____
_____
_____

Meditation:

In my desperation I prayed, and the Lord listened; he saved me from all
my troubles.
(Psalm 34:6)

Revelations

What is being revealed to you? How has God shown up in your life?

_____

_____

_____

_____

_____

_____

_____

_____

_____

_____

_____

_____

_____

_____

_____

_____

_____

_____

_____

_____

_____

_____

_____

_____

_____

_____

_____

_____

He was the one who prayed to the God of Israel, "Oh, that you would bless me and expand my territory! Please be with me in all that I do, and keep me from all trouble and pain!" And God granted him his request.
(1 Chronicles 4:10)

Chapter Eight

Privilege

Reading:

Don't be intimidated in any way by your enemies. This will be a sign to them that they are going to be destroyed, but that you are going to be saved, even by God himself.

For you have been given not only the privilege of trusting in Christ, but also the privilege of suffering for him.

We are in this struggle together. You have seen my struggle in the past, and you know that I am still in the midst of it.
(Philippians 1:28-30)

Privilege

Day 26

Call to Action:

Today, notice all the privileges you have that others may not have.

What are you taking for granted in your life?

How can you share your privileges with others?

"Life is a privilege" filled with many opportunities for growth. Some opportunities may be seen as a test, chaos or crisis. But they are merely openings on the journey of life to receive more of God's blessings, favor and grace.

Reflection:

_____

_____

_____

_____

_____

_____

_____

_____

_____

_____

Privilege

Prayer:

The Lord is my shepherd; I have all that I need. He lets me rest in green
meadows; he leads me beside peaceful streams. He renews my strength.
He guides me along right paths, bringing honor to his name. Even when
I walk through the darkest valley, I will not be afraid, for you are close
besides me. Your rod and your staff protect and comfort me. You prepare
a feast for me in the presence of my enemies. You honor me by anointing
my head with oil. Surely your goodness and unfailing love will pursue
me all the days of my life, and I will live in the house of the Lord forever.
(Psalm 23:1-6)

Prayer Journal
God is never silent. He is always speaking to you . . . Be still and listen.

_____

_____

_____

_____

_____

_____

_____

_____

_____

_____

Meditation:

In my desperation I prayed, and the Lord listened; he saved me from all
my troubles.
(Psalm 34:6)

Love

Day 27

Reading:

I pray that from his glorious, unlimited resources he will empower you with inner strength through his Spirit.

Then Christ will make his home in your hearts as you trust in him. Your roots will grow down into God's love and keep you strong.

And may you have the power to understand, as all God's people should, how wide, how long, how high, and how deep his love is.

May you experience the love of Christ, though it is too great to understand fully. Then you will be made complete with all the fullness of life and power that comes from God.

Now all glory to God, who is able, through his mighty power at work within us, to accomplish infinitely more than we might ask or think.
(Ephesians 3:16-20)

Love

Call to Action:

Today, tell five people that you love them. Be sincere and authentic—it may feel a little weird at first but press through the task. Love is the key to our salvation.

People often have a tendency to express love and gratitude through material possessions. It is time to change this scenario! Nothing is more valuable than telling someone you love them (face to face or voice to voice), forgo the texing, posting, leaving a message or instant messenger—no social media required or allowed.

Write down how you felt after expressing your love and how it was received.

Reflection:

_____
_____
_____
_____
_____
_____
_____
_____
_____
_____

Love

Prayer:

The Lord is my shepherd; I have all that I need. He lets me rest in green
meadows; he leads me beside peaceful streams. He renews my strength.
He guides me along right paths, bringing honor to his name. Even when
I walk through the darkest valley, I will not be afraid, for you are close
besides me. Your rod and your staff protect and comfort me. You prepare
a feast for me in the presence of my enemies. You honor me by anointing
my head with oil. Surely your goodness and unfailing love will pursue
me all the days of my life, and I will live in the house of the Lord forever.
(Psalm 23:1-6)

Prayer Journal
God is never silent. He is always speaking to you . . . Be still and listen.

_____
_____
_____
_____
_____
_____
_____
_____
_____
_____

Meditation:

In my desperation I prayed, and the Lord listened; he saved me from all
my troubles.
(Psalm 34:6)

Test

Reading:

When the people heard the thunder and the loud blast of the ram's horn, and when they saw the flashes of lightning and the smoke billowing from the mountain, they stood at a distance, trembling with fear.

And they said to Moses, "You speak to us, and we will listen. But don't let God speak directly to us, or we will die!"

"Don't be afraid," Moses answered them, "for God has come in this way to test you, and so that your fear of him will keep you from sinning!"

As the people stood in the distance, Moses approached the dark cloud where God was.
(Exodus 20:18-21)

Test

Day 28

Call to Action:

Today, if your situation were a test of your faith in God, would you pass or fail?

What could you be doing better or differently?

Sometimes what is the appearance of a test is really an anointing of responsibility and the awaiting achievement of what is to be expressed through your testimony.

Reflection:

_____
_____
_____
_____
_____
_____
_____
_____
_____
_____

Test

Day 28

Prayer:

The Lord is my shepherd; I have all that I need. He lets me rest in green meadows; he leads me beside peaceful streams. He renews my strength. He guides me along right paths, bringing honor to his name. Even when I walk through the darkest valley, I will not be afraid, for you are close besides me. Your rod and your staff protect and comfort me. You prepare a feast for me in the presence of my enemies. You honor me by anointing my head with oil. Surely your goodness and unfailing love will pursue me all the days of my life, and I will live in the house of the Lord forever.
(Psalm 23:1-6)

Prayer Journal
God is never silent. He is always speaking to you . . . Be still and listen.

_____

_____

_____

_____

_____

_____

_____

_____

_____

_____

Meditation:

In my desperation I prayed, and the Lord listened; he saved me from all my troubles.
(Psalm 34:6)

More Than

Day 29

Reading:

Then, turning to his disciples, Jesus said, "That is why I tell you not
to worry about everyday life—whether you have enough food to eat or
enough clothes to wear.

For life is more than food, and your body more than clothing.

Look at the ravens. They don't plant or harvest or store food in barns, for
God feeds them. And you are far more valuable to him than any birds!

Can all your worries add a single moment to your life?

And if worry can't accomplish a little thing like that, what's the use of
worrying over bigger things?
(Luke 12:22-26)

More Than

Day 29

Call to Action:

Today, what if your life were "more than" you could ever imagine it to be? How would you describe it? Where would you live? What car would you be driving? Would you still seek God first?

What if all things were possible for you—no limits, how would your life be different?

God is waiting to bless you with the full Stewardship and keys to hidden treasures. The mind cannot conceive the endless possibilities . . . more than you could ever imagine.

Reflection:

_____

_____

_____

_____

_____

_____

_____

_____

_____

_____

More Than

Day 29

Prayer:

The Lord is my shepherd; I have all that I need. He lets me rest in green meadows; he leads me beside peaceful streams. He renews my strength. He guides me along right paths, bringing honor to his name. Even when I walk through the darkest valley, I will not be afraid, for you are close besides me. Your rod and your staff protect and comfort me. You prepare a feast for me in the presence of my enemies. You honor me by anointing my head with oil. Surely your goodness and unfailing love will pursue me all the days of my life, and I will live in the house of the Lord forever.
(Psalm 23:1-6)

Prayer Journal
God is never silent. He is always speaking to you . . . Be still and listen.

_____
_____
_____
_____
_____
_____
_____
_____
_____
_____

Meditation:

In my desperation I prayed, and the Lord listened; he saved me from all my troubles.
(Psalm 34:6)

Joy

Reading:

"I have loved you even as the Father has loved me. Remain in my love.

When you obey my commandments, you remain in my love, just as I obey my Father's commandments and remain in his love.

I have told you these things so that you will be filled with my joy. Yes, your joy will overflow!

This is my commandment: Love each other in the same way I have loved you.

There is no greater love than to lay down one's life for one's friends.

You are my friends if you do what I command.
(John 15:9-14)

Joy

Call to Action:

Today, find joy in your situation. Know that time and place are only part of a season. And this too shall pass . . . Joy is an emotion that is always available to us.

Count the moments in the day you experience or express joy. If less than ten, you have plenty of work to do to increase the joy in your life. Simple pleasures are often the easiest to experience in this economy.

Reflection:

_____
_____
_____
_____
_____
_____
_____
_____
_____
_____

Joy

Prayer:

The Lord is my shepherd; I have all that I need. He lets me rest in green
meadows; he leads me beside peaceful streams. He renews my strength.
He guides me along right paths, bringing honor to his name. Even when
I walk through the darkest valley, I will not be afraid, for you are close
besides me. Your rod and your staff protect and comfort me. You prepare
a feast for me in the presence of my enemies. You honor me by anointing
my head with oil. Surely your goodness and unfailing love will pursue
me all the days of my life, and I will live in the house of the Lord forever.
(Psalm 23:1-6)

Prayer Journal
God is never silent. He is always speaking to you . . . Be still and listen.

_____
_____
_____
_____
_____
_____
_____
_____
_____
_____

Meditation:

In my desperation I prayed, and the Lord listened; he saved me from all
my troubles.
(Psalm 34:6)

Revelations

What is being revealed to you? How has God shown up in your life?

_____

_____

_____

_____

_____

_____

_____

_____

_____

_____

_____

_____

_____

_____

_____

_____

_____

_____

_____

_____

_____

_____

_____

_____

_____

_____

_____

_____

_____

_____

He was the one who prayed to the God of Israel, "Oh, that you would bless me and expand my territory! Please be with me in all that I do, and keep me from all trouble and pain!" And God granted him his request.
(1 Chronicles 4:10)

Chapter Nine

Dread

Reading:

> The LORD has given me a strong warning not to think like everyone else does. He said,
>
> Don't call everything a conspiracy, like they do, and don't live in dread of what frightens them.
>
> Make the LORD of Heaven's Armies holy in your life. He is the one you should fear. He is the one who should make you tremble.
>
> He will keep you safe.
> (Isaiah 8:11-14)

Dread

Day 31

Call to Action:

Today, do something that you have been dreading. Do it and get it done and over with. Surely, a moment of accomplishment is better than a lifetime of dreadful memories or missed opportunities.

Dread anchors you to regret, and regret is like a cancer to your soul. A moment of a dreaded action could be just the dose you need to preventing cancer and other attacks being raged against you. And if not, at least you can say you did it . . . and now check the task off your to do list.

Reflection:

_____

_____

_____

_____

_____

_____

_____

_____

_____

_____

Dread

Prayer:

The Lord is my shepherd; I have all that I need. He lets me rest in green
meadows; he leads me beside peaceful streams. He renews my strength.
He guides me along right paths, bringing honor to his name. Even when
I walk through the darkest valley, I will not be afraid, for you are close
besides me. Your rod and your staff protect and comfort me. You prepare
a feast for me in the presence of my enemies. You honor me by anointing
my head with oil. Surely your goodness and unfailing love will pursue
me all the days of my life, and I will live in the house of the Lord forever.
(Psalm 23:1-6)

Prayer Journal
God is never silent. He is always speaking to you . . . Be still and listen.

Meditation:

Trust in the Lord with all your heart; do not depend on your own
understanding. Seek his will in all you do, and he will show you which
path to take.
(Proverbs 3:5-6)

Secret Riches

Day 32

Reading:

This is what the LORD says to Cyrus, his anointed one, whose right hand
he will empower. Before him, mighty kings will be paralyzed with fear.
Their fortress gates will be opened, never to shut again.

This is what the LORD says: "I will go before you, Cyrus, and
level the mountains.

I will smash down gates of bronze and cut through bars of iron.

And I will give you treasures hidden in the darkness—secret riches. I will
do this so you may know that I am the LORD, the God of Israel, the one
who calls you by name.
(Isaiah 45:1-3)

Secret Riches

Call to Action:

Today, explore your secret riches, better known as your talents. Make a list of all the things you are talented at doing. Make another list of all the things you wish you had talent in and start to pursue them passionately!

Upon conception, we all received our secret riches and as we grow, some are discovered, misused, or wasted away yet the greatest of all riches is yet to be unveiled.

Reflection:

_____
_____
_____
_____
_____
_____
_____
_____
_____
_____

Secret Riches

Day 32

Prayer:

The Lord is my shepherd; I have all that I need. He lets me rest in green meadows; he leads me beside peaceful streams. He renews my strength. He guides me along right paths, bringing honor to his name. Even when I walk through the darkest valley, I will not be afraid, for you are close besides me. Your rod and your staff protect and comfort me. You prepare a feast for me in the presence of my enemies. You honor me by anointing my head with oil. Surely your goodness and unfailing love will pursue me all the days of my life, and I will live in the house of the Lord forever.
(Psalm 23:1-6)

Prayer Journal
God is never silent. He is always speaking to you . . . Be still and listen.

_____
_____
_____
_____
_____
_____
_____
_____
_____
_____

Meditation:

Trust in the Lord with all your heart; do not depend on your own understanding. Seek his will in all you do, and he will show you which path to take.
(Proverbs 3:5-6)

Will Not Consume You

Day 33

Reading:

But now, O Jacob, listen to the LORD who created you. O Israel, the one who formed you says, "Do not be afraid, for I have ransomed you. I have called you by name; you are mine.

When you go through deep waters, I will be with you. When you go through rivers of difficulty, you will not drown. When you walk through the fire of oppression, you will not be burned up; the flames will not consume you.

For I am the LORD, your God, the Holy One of Israel, your Savior. I gave Egypt as a ransom for your freedom; I gave Ethiopia and Seba in your place.

Others were given in exchange for you. I traded their lives for yours because you are precious to me. You are honored, and I love you.
(Isaiah 43:1-4)

Will Not Consume You

Day 33

Call to Action:

Today, take an inventory of what you are consumed with, i.e., thoughts, a person, situation, money, food, keeping up an appearance, finding a job, or losing your home. For everything that may be consuming your attention, write down a positive statement or affirmation describing your feelings.

Example: I can not find a job. Affirmation: Employment doors are now opening all around me. I am qualified and ready to accept my new position, right now.

Every situation has a positive and a negative; it is our focus that manifests the attraction to either one.

Reflection:

_____

_____

_____

_____

_____

_____

_____

_____

_____

Will Not Consume You

Prayer:

The Lord is my shepherd; I have all that I need. He lets me rest in green
meadows; he leads me beside peaceful streams. He renews my strength.
He guides me along right paths, bringing honor to his name. Even when
I walk through the darkest valley, I will not be afraid, for you are close
besides me. Your rod and your staff protect and comfort me. You prepare
a feast for me in the presence of my enemies. You honor me by anointing
my head with oil. Surely your goodness and unfailing love will pursue
me all the days of my life, and I will live in the house of the Lord forever.
(Psalm 23:1-6)

Prayer Journal
God is never silent. He is always speaking to you . . . Be still and listen.

_____
_____
_____
_____
_____
_____
_____
_____
_____
_____

Meditation:

Trust in the Lord with all your heart; do not depend on your own
understanding. Seek his will in all you do, and he will show you which
path to take.
(Proverbs 3:5-6)

Kingdom of God

Day 34

Reading:

> Look at the lilies and how they grow. They don't work or make
> their clothing, yet Solomon in all his glory was not dressed as
> beautifully as they are.
>
> And if God cares so wonderfully for flowers that are here today and
> thrown into the fire tomorrow, he will certainly care for you. Why do you
> have so little faith?
>
> "And don't be concerned about what to eat and what to drink. Don't
> worry about such things.
>
> These things dominate the thoughts of unbelievers all over the world, but
> your Father already knows your needs.
>
> Seek the Kingdom of God above all else, and he will give you
> everything you need.
>
> "So don't be afraid, little flock. For it gives your Father great happiness to
> give you the Kingdom.
> (Luke 12:27-32)

Kingdom of God

Day 34

Call to Action:

Today, take a walk and count all the blessings around you. With every step, envision yourself as walking through the Kingdom of God. What would that feel like?

Know that each day you can take a journey walking through God's Kingdom here on earth by enjoying the trees, birds, grass, sand, or sea.

Behold the greatness and vastness of God's ability. Know if He created the heavens and earth, He can certainly take care of your needs.

See God in everything around you.

Reflection:

_____

_____

_____

_____

_____

_____

_____

_____

_____

_____

Kingdom of God

Prayer:

The Lord is my shepherd; I have all that I need. He lets me rest in green
meadows; he leads me beside peaceful streams. He renews my strength.
He guides me along right paths, bringing honor to his name. Even when
I walk through the darkest valley, I will not be afraid, for you are close
besides me. Your rod and your staff protect and comfort me. You prepare
a feast for me in the presence of my enemies. You honor me by anointing
my head with oil. Surely your goodness and unfailing love will pursue
me all the days of my life, and I will live in the house of the Lord forever.
(Psalm 23:1-6)

Prayer Journal
God is never silent. He is always speaking to you . . . Be still and listen.

_____

_____

_____

_____

_____

_____

_____

_____

_____

_____

Meditation:

Trust in the Lord with all your heart; do not depend on your own
understanding. Seek his will in all you do, and he will show you which
path to take.
(Proverbs 3:5-6)

Peace

Day 35

Reading:

Always be full of joy in the Lord. I say it again—rejoice!

Let everyone see that you are considerate in all you do. Remember, the Lord is coming soon.

Don't worry about anything; instead, pray about everything. Tell God what you need, and thank him for all he has done.

Then you will experience God's peace, which exceeds anything we can understand. His peace will guard your hearts and minds as you live in Christ Jesus.
(Philippians 4:4-7)

Peace

Day 35

Call to Action:

Today, make peace with someone from your past. Power can be delivered through peace.

Pray that your offering of peace is accepted with open hands and a gentle spirit. Regardless of the outcome, you will be rewarded for your efforts.

It does not matter who forgives first, but the one who never forgives will surely lose.

Think about making frequent deposits of peace in your Soul-Bank.

Reflection:

_____

_____

_____

_____

_____

_____

_____

_____

_____

Peace

Prayer:

The Lord is my shepherd; I have all that I need. He lets me rest in green
meadows; he leads me beside peaceful streams. He renews my strength.
He guides me along right paths, bringing honor to his name. Even when
I walk through the darkest valley, I will not be afraid, for you are close
besides me. Your rod and your staff protect and comfort me. You prepare
a feast for me in the presence of my enemies. You honor me by anointing
my head with oil. Surely your goodness and unfailing love will pursue
me all the days of my life, and I will live in the house of the Lord forever.
(Psalm 23:1-6)

Prayer Journal
God is never silent. He is always speaking to you . . . Be still and listen.

_____
_____
_____
_____
_____
_____
_____
_____
_____
_____

Meditation:

Trust in the Lord with all your heart; do not depend on your own
understanding. Seek his will in all you do, and he will show you which
path to take.
(Proverbs 3:5-6)

Revelations

What is being revealed to you? How has God shown up in your life?

_____

_____

_____

_____

_____

_____

_____

_____

_____

_____

_____

_____

_____

_____

_____

_____

_____

_____

_____

_____

_____

_____

_____

_____

_____

He was the one who prayed to the God of Israel, "Oh, that you would bless me and expand my territory! Please be with me in all that I do, and keep me from all trouble and pain!" And God granted him his request.
(1 Chronicles 4:10)

Chapter Ten

Give

Day 36

Reading:

Love your enemies! Do good to them. Lend to them without expecting to be repaid. Then your reward from heaven will be very great, and you will truly be acting as children of the Most High, for he is kind to those who are unthankful and wicked.

You must be compassionate, just as your Father is compassionate.

"Do not judge others, and you will not be judged. Do not condemn others, or it will all come back against you. Forgive others, and you will be forgiven.

Give, and you will receive. Your gift will return to you in full—pressed down, shaken together to make room for more, running over, and poured into your lap. The amount you give will determine the amount you get back.
(Luke 6:35-38)

Give

Call to Action:

Today, find someone you can assist, volunteer or get involved with a cause or local charity. One act, one intention, one person can impact the lives of many.

A closed hand is not only closed to giving but to receiving as well.

Reflection:

_____
_____
_____
_____
_____
_____
_____
_____
_____
_____

Give

Prayer:

The Lord is my shepherd; I have all that I need. He lets me rest in green
meadows; he leads me beside peaceful streams. He renews my strength.
He guides me along right paths, bringing honor to his name. Even when
I walk through the darkest valley, I will not be afraid, for you are close
besides me. Your rod and your staff protect and comfort me. You prepare
a feast for me in the presence of my enemies. You honor me by anointing
my head with oil. Surely your goodness and unfailing love will pursue
me all the days of my life, and I will live in the house of the Lord forever.
(Psalm 23:1-6)

Prayer Journal
God is never silent. He is always speaking to you . . . Be still and listen.

_____

_____

_____

_____

_____

_____

_____

_____

_____

_____

Meditation:

Trust in the Lord with all your heart; do not depend on your own
understanding. Seek his will in all you do, and he will show you which
path to take.
(Proverbs 3:5-6)

Supply

Day 37

Reading:

At the moment I have all I need—and more! I am generously supplied with the gifts you sent me with Epaphroditus. They are a sweet-smelling sacrifice that is acceptable and pleasing to God.

And this same God who takes care of me will supply all your needs from his glorious riches, which have been given to us in Christ Jesus.

Now all glory to God our Father forever and ever! Amen
(Philippians 4:18-20)

Supply

Day 37

Call to Action:

Today, turn off all sources of negativity and identify several of your favorite songs and play them repeatedly and watch the negativity disapate. Make a list of 5 favorite tunes and emotions felt when you are listening to them. Let music be your secret supply when you need a release. Music feeds the soul and warms the heart.

Reflection:

_____

_____

_____

_____

_____

_____

_____

_____

_____

_____

Supply

Day 37

Prayer:

The Lord is my shepherd; I have all that I need. He lets me rest in green
meadows; he leads me beside peaceful streams. He renews my strength.
He guides me along right paths, bringing honor to his name. Even when
I walk through the darkest valley, I will not be afraid, for you are close
besides me. Your rod and your staff protect and comfort me. You prepare
a feast for me in the presence of my enemies. You honor me by anointing
my head with oil. Surely your goodness and unfailing love will pursue
me all the days of my life, and I will live in the house of the Lord forever.
(Psalm 23:1-6)

Prayer Journal
God is never silent. He is always speaking to you . . . Be still and listen.

_____

_____

_____

_____

_____

_____

_____

_____

_____

_____

Meditation:

Trust in the Lord with all your heart; do not depend on your own
understanding. Seek his will in all you do, and he will show you which
path to take.
(Proverbs 3:5-6)

Work

Reading:

And the Holy Spirit helps us in our weakness. For example, we don't know what God wants us to pray for. But the Holy Spirit prays for us with groanings that cannot be expressed in words.

And the Father who knows all hearts knows what the Spirit is saying, for the Spirit pleads for us believers[c] in harmony with God's own will.

And we know that God causes everything to work together for the good of those who love God and are called according to his purpose for them (Romans 8:26-28)

Work

Day 38

Call to Action:

Today, make a list of the things working in your life and work harder at them. We can always improve or learn something new. If you are good at something, perfect it and then share or teach it to another.

Anytime you give to aid another you will elevate your life's work on this planet.

Reflection:

_____

_____

_____

_____

_____

_____

_____

_____

_____

_____

Work

Prayer:

The Lord is my shepherd; I have all that I need. He lets me rest in green
meadows; he leads me beside peaceful streams. He renews my strength.
He guides me along right paths, bringing honor to his name. Even when
I walk through the darkest valley, I will not be afraid, for you are close
besides me. Your rod and your staff protect and comfort me. You prepare
a feast for me in the presence of my enemies. You honor me by anointing
my head with oil. Surely your goodness and unfailing love will pursue
me all the days of my life, and I will live in the house of the Lord forever.
(Psalm 23:1-6)

Prayer Journal
God is never silent. He is always speaking to you . . . Be still and listen.

_____
_____
_____
_____
_____
_____
_____
_____
_____
_____

Meditation:

Trust in the Lord with all your heart; do not depend on your own
understanding. Seek his will in all you do, and he will show you which
path to take.
(Proverbs 3:5-6)

Separate

Reading:

And I am convinced that nothing can ever separate us from God's love. Neither death nor life, neither angels nor demons, neither our fears for today nor our worries about tomorrow—not even the powers of hell can separate us from God's love.

No power in the sky above or in the earth below—indeed, nothing in all creation will ever be able to separate us from the love of God that is revealed in Christ Jesus our Lord.
(Romans 8:38-39)

Separate

Call to Action:

Today, separate your efforts and thoughts into good and bad. Reflect on the amount of bad efforts or thoughts and see how you can turn them into positive ones. Each time a bad thought or a situation comes up, ask yourself; how can I separate myself from this situation and honor God?

Reflection:

_____

_____

_____

_____

_____

_____

_____

_____

_____

_____

Separate

Prayer:

The Lord is my shepherd; I have all that I need. He lets me rest in green meadows; he leads me beside peaceful streams. He renews my strength. He guides me along right paths, bringing honor to his name. Even when I walk through the darkest valley, I will not be afraid, for you are close besides me. Your rod and your staff protect and comfort me. You prepare a feast for me in the presence of my enemies. You honor me by anointing my head with oil. Surely your goodness and unfailing love will pursue me all the days of my life, and I will live in the house of the Lord forever.
(Psalm 23:1-6)

Prayer Journal
God is never silent. He is always speaking to you . . . Be still and listen.

_____
_____
_____
_____
_____
_____
_____
_____
_____

Meditation:

Trust in the Lord with all your heart; do not depend on your own understanding. Seek his will in all you do, and he will show you which path to take.
(Proverbs 3:5-6)

Stretched Out

Day 40

Reading:

God, the LORD, created the heavens and stretched them out. He created
the earth and everything in it. He gives breath to everyone, life to
everyone who walks the earth. And it is he who says,

"I, the LORD, have called you to demonstrate my righteousness. I will take
you by the hand and guard you, and I will give you to my people, Israel,
as a symbol of my covenant with them. And you will be a light to guide
the nations.

You will open the eyes of the blind. You will free the captives from prison,
releasing those who sit in dark dungeons.

"I am the LORD; that is my name! I will not give my glory to anyone else,
nor share my praise with carved idols.

Everything I prophesied has come true, and now I will prophesy again.

I will tell you the future before it happens."

Sing a new song to the LORD! Sing his praises from the ends of the earth!

Sing, all you who sail the seas, all you who live in distant coastlands.
(Isaiah 42:5-10)

Stretched Out

Call to Action:

Today, allow yourself to stretch past your routine thinking. Write down a list of forty things you want to accomplish as if there are no limits to what you can achieve or experience! Then meditate on each thing on your list, regularly and *see* what is possible for you and your life. Dare to dream big!

Reflection:

_____

_____

_____

_____

_____

_____

_____

_____

_____

Stretched Out

Day 40

Prayer:

The Lord is my shepherd; I have all that I need. He lets me rest in green meadows; he leads me beside peaceful streams. He renews my strength. He guides me along right paths, bringing honor to his name. Even when I walk through the darkest valley, I will not be afraid, for you are close besides me. Your rod and your staff protect and comfort me. You prepare a feast for me in the presence of my enemies. You honor me by anointing my head with oil. Surely your goodness and unfailing love will pursue me all the days of my life, and I will live in the house of the Lord forever.
(Psalm 23:1-6)

Prayer Journal
God is never silent. He is always speaking to you . . . Be still and listen.

_____

_____

_____

_____

_____

_____

_____

_____

_____

_____

Meditation:

Trust in the Lord with all your heart; do not depend on your own understanding. Seek his will in all you do, and he will show you which path to take.
(Proverbs 3:-6)

Revelations

What is being revealed to you? How has God shown up in your life?

_____

_____

_____

_____

_____

_____

_____

_____

_____

_____

_____

_____

_____

_____

_____

_____

_____

_____

_____

_____

_____

_____

_____

_____

_____

_____

_____

_____

He was the one who prayed to the God of Israel, "Oh, that you would bless me and expand my territory! Please be with me in all that I do, and keep me from all trouble and pain!" And God granted him his request.
(1 Chronicles 4:10)

Chapter Eleven

God's Answers

Addiction

Jesus replied, "I tell you the truth, everyone who sins is a slave to sin. Now a slave has no permanent place in the family, but a son belongs to it forever. So if the Son sets you free, you will be free indeed.
(John 8:34-36)

Anxiety

Let the peace of Christ rule in your hearts, since as members of one body you were called to peace. And be thankful.
(Colossians 3:15)

Burdens

Give your burdens to the LORD, and he will take care of you. He will not permit the godly to slip and fall.
(Psalm 55:22)

Complaining

These people are grumblers and complainers, living only to satisfy their desires. They brag loudly about themselves, and they flatter others to get what they want.
(Jude 16-20)

Confusion

For God is not a God of disorder but of peace. As in all the congregations of the saints,

(1 Corinthians 14:33)

Courage

Have I not commanded you? Be strong and courageous. Do not be terrified; do not be discouraged, for the LORD your God will be with you wherever you go."

(Joshua 1:9)

Debts

She went and told the man of God, and he said, "Go, sell the oil and pay your debts. You and your sons can live on what is left."

(2 Kings 4:7)

Deliverance

You, dear children, are from God and have overcome them, because the one who is in you is greater than the one who is in the world.

(1 John 4:4)

God's Answers

Depression

Why are you downcast, O my soul? Why so disturbed within me? Put your hope in God, for I will yet praise him, my Savior and my God. My soul is downcast within me; therefore I will remember you from the land of the Jordan, the heights of Hermon—from Mount Mizar.
(Psalm 42:5-6)

Divorce

But for those who are married, I have a command that comes not from me, but from the Lord. A wife must not leave her husband. But if she does leave him, let her remain single or else be reconciled to him. And the husband must not leave his wife.
(1 Corinthians 7:10-11)

Employment

Pay careful attention to your own work, for then you will get the satisfaction of a job well done, and you won't need to compare yourself to anyone else. For we are each responsible for our own conduct.
(Galatians 6:4-5)

Forgiveness

If we confess our sins, he is faithful and just and will forgive us our sins and purify us from all unrighteousness.
(1 John 1:9)

Fear

My child, don't lose sight of common sense and discernment. Hang on to them, for they will refresh your soul. They are like jewels on a necklace. They keep you safe on your way, and your feet will not stumble. You can go to bed without fear; you will lie down and sleep soundly. You need not be afraid of sudden disaster of the destruction that comes upon the wicked, for the Lord is your security. He will keep your foot from being caught in a trap.
(Proverbs 3:21-26)

Greed

Look here, you rich people: Weep and groan with anguish because of all the terrible troubles ahead of you. Your wealth is rotting away, and your fine clothes are moth-eaten rags. Your gold and silver have become worthless. The very wealth you were counting on will eat away your flesh like fire. This treasure you have accumulated will stand as evidence against you on the day of judgment. For listen! Hear the cries of the field workers whom you have cheated of their pay. The wages you held back cry out against you. The cries of those who harvest your fields have reached the ears of the LORD of Heaven's Armies. You have spent your years on earth in luxury, satisfying your every desire. You have fattened yourselves for the day of slaughter.

(James 5:1-5)

Hope

For everything that was written in the past was written to teach us, so that through endurance and the encouragement of the Scriptures we might have hope.

(Romans 15:4)

God's Answers

Isolation / Loneliness

I will not leave you as orphans; I will come to you.
(John 14:18)

Loss

But whatever was to my profit I now consider loss for the sake of Christ.
What is more, I consider everything a loss compared to the surpassing
greatness of knowing Christ Jesus my Lord, for whose sake I have lost all
things. I consider them rubbish, that I may gain Christ
(Philippians 3:7-8)

Material possessions

A good person produces good things from the treasury of a good heart, and
an evil person produces evil things from the treasury of an evil heart. What
you say flows from what is in your heart.
(Luke 6:45)

Money

For the love of money is the root of all kinds of evil. And some people,
craving money, have wandered from the true faith and pierced themselves
with many sorrows.
(1 Timothy 6:10)

Patients

The Lord isn't really being slow about his promise, as some people think.
No, he is being patient for your sake. He does not want anyone to be
destroyed, but wants everyone to repent.
(2 Peter 3:9)

Protection

But you are a shield around me, O LORD; you bestow glory on me and lift up my head.

(Psalm 3:3)

Recession

Then we cried out to the LORD, the God of our fathers, and the LORD heard our voice and saw our misery, toil and oppression.

(Deuteronomy. 26:7)

Sowing and Tithing

Remember this: Whoever sows sparingly will also reap sparingly, and whoever sows generously will also reap generously. Each man should give what he has decided in his heart to give, not reluctantly or under compulsion, for God loves a cheerful giver. And God is able to make all grace abound to you, so that in all things at all times, having all that you need, you will abound in every good work.

(2 Corinthians 9:6-8)

God's Answers

Stress
Cast your cares on the LORD and he will sustain you; he will never let the righteous fall.
(Psalm 55:22)

Suicide
"But cowards, unbelievers, the corrupt, murderers, the immoral, those who practice witchcraft, idol worshipers, and all liars—their fate is in the fiery lake of burning sulfur. This is the second death."
(Revelations 21:8)

Temptation
And remember, when you are being tempted, do not say, "God is tempting me." God is never tempted to do wrong, and he never tempts anyone else. Temptation comes from our own desires, which entice us and drag us away. These desires give birth to sinful actions. And when sin is allowed to grow, it gives birth to death.
(James 1:13-15)

Violence
Now God saw that the earth had become corrupt and was filled with violence. God observed all this corruption in the world, for everyone on earth was corrupt. So God said to Noah, "I have decided to destroy all living creatures, for they have filled the earth with violence. Yes, I will wipe them all out along with the earth!
(Genesis 6:11-14)

Wealth
And this same God who takes care of me will supply all your needs from his glorious riches, which have been given to us in Christ Jesus.
(Philippians 4:19)

Worry
So humble yourselves under the mighty power of God, and at the right time he will lift you up in honor. Give all your worries and cares to God, for he cares about you
(1 Peter 5:6-7)

Chapter Twelve

Journal

_____

_____

_____

_____

_____

_____

_____

_____

_____

_____

_____

_____

_____

_____

_____

_____

_____

_____

_____

_____

_____

_____

_____

Journal

Journal

Journal

Journal

Journal

Journal

_____
_____
_____
_____
_____
_____
_____
_____
_____
_____
_____
_____
_____
_____
_____
_____
_____
_____
_____
_____
_____
_____
_____
_____
_____
_____
_____
_____
_____

Journal

_____
_____
_____
_____
_____
_____
_____
_____
_____
_____
_____
_____
_____
_____
_____
_____
_____
_____
_____
_____
_____
_____
_____
_____
_____
_____
_____
_____
_____
_____

Journal

Journal

_____
_____
_____
_____
_____
_____
_____
_____
_____
_____
_____
_____
_____
_____
_____
_____
_____
_____
_____
_____
_____
_____
_____
_____
_____
_____
_____
_____

Journal

Scriptural Index

Intermedia Publishing Group

Publishing That Works For You

Do you need a speaker?

Do you want Zena Contreras to speak to your group or event? Then contact Larry Davis at: **(623) 337-8710** or email: **ldavis@intermediapr.com** or use the contact form at: **www.intermediapr.com**.

Whether you want to purchase bulk copies of *40 Day Living* or buy another book for a friend, get it now at: **www.imprbooks.com**.

If you have a book that you would like to publish, contact Larry Davis, Publisher, at Intermedia Publishing Group, (623) 337-8710 or email: ldavis@intermediapr.com or use the contact form at: www.intermediapub.com.